ARCTIC ANIMAL
FOOD CHAINS

WRITTEN BY
Jordan Hoffman

Everything in an environment is connected.

Think about a polar bear eating a ringed seal. Before that, the ringed seal was eating Arctic cod. And the Arctic cod need to eat, too!

These connections can be shown in a diagram called a food chain.

What Is a Food Chain?

A food chain shows how energy moves from one living thing to the next. Living things get their energy from food.

The first link in a food chain is usually a plant. Most plants use energy from the sun to make their own food.

The second link is an animal that eats the plant. The third link is an animal that eats the animal in the second link. In each link, the animal eats the living thing that came before it.

wolf eats
caribou

caribou eats
cotton grass

5

Bylot Island

Food chains exist anywhere that there are living things.

Let's look at a food chain on Bylot Island, Nunavut. Bylot Island is near the community of Mittimatalik. In this food chain, you will find grasses, snow geese, Arctic foxes, and snowy owls.

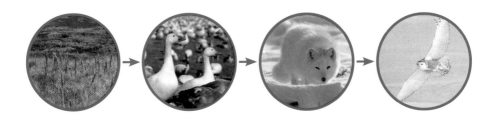

Grasses

Let's start at the bottom of a food chain on Bylot Island and work our way up.

Grasses are the **first link** in this Bylot Island food chain. They grow all over the tundra in Nunavut. Grasses use sunlight to make sugars, and they use the sugars as food.

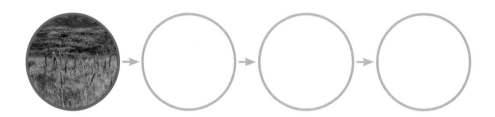

Snow Geese

Snow geese are the **second link** in this Bylot Island food chain. Snow geese live in groups called colonies. A huge colony of snow geese lives on Bylot Island. It has up to 100,000 geese!

The snow geese eat the grasses on the island. You can imagine how much grass is needed to feed that many snow geese!

Arctic Foxes

Arctic foxes are the **third link** in this Bylot Island food chain. They eat snow goose eggs and young snow geese.

Adult snow geese try to defend their nests from Arctic foxes. This makes it harder for a fox to get food. If Arctic foxes can't get enough snow geese to eat, they might not be able to have babies. Then there are fewer foxes on Bylot Island.

Snowy Owls

Snowy owls are the **final link** of this Bylot Island food chain. Snowy owls are skilled hunters. They use their long, sharp talons to catch other animals to eat.

Snowy owls eat animals below them in the food chain, including snow geese and young Arctic foxes. Some snowy owls can even hunt adult foxes, but they are harder to catch!

What happens when one link in the food chain is taken out?

When one link in the food chain is taken out, the number of plants or animals connected to that link might change.

For example, if there were no snow geese on Bylot Island, there might be more grass because the geese wouldn't be eating it. But the Arctic foxes might disappear because they would not have any snow geese to eat. Without any foxes, the snowy owls might disappear, too!

Lake Hazen

The Bylot Island food chain shows how living things eat other living things on the land. Food chains also exist in the water.

This is Lake Hazen, on Ellesmere Island in Nunavut. Let's look at the Lake Hazen food chain to see how living things in the lake are connected.

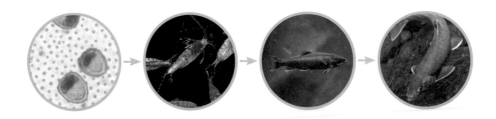

Algae

In Lake Hazen, the first link in the food chain is algae. Algae are tiny plants. They are so small that you often need a microscope to see them in the water.

Algae grow under the ice in lakes in the spring and in open water in summer. Just like grasses on the tundra, algae use sunlight to make food.

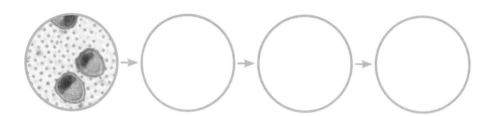

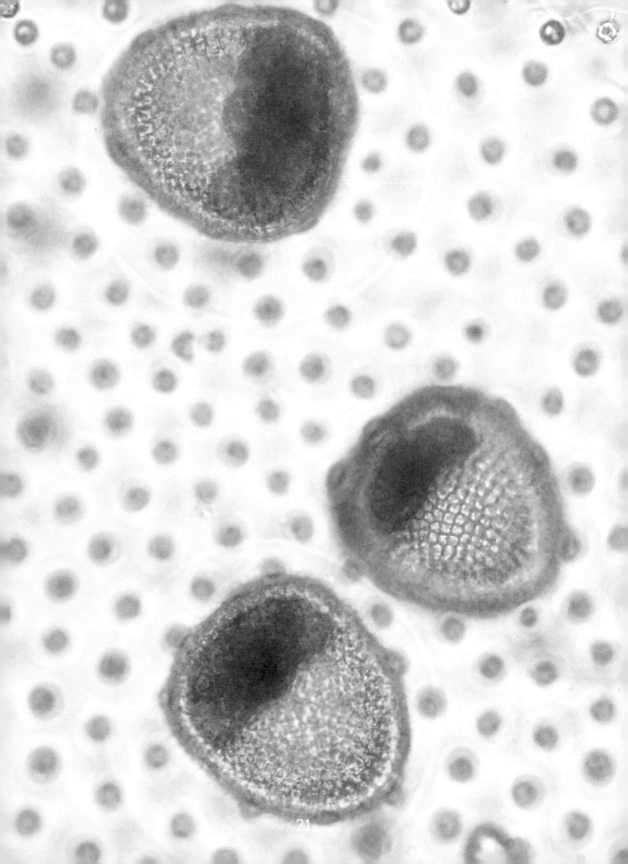

Copepods

The second link in the Lake Hazen food chain is the copepod. Copepods are very tiny animals. They look like small shrimp.

There are a lot of copepods in Lake Hazen. They eat the algae in the lake.

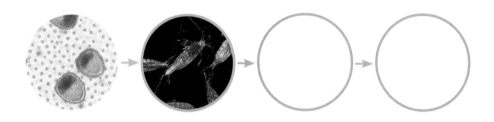

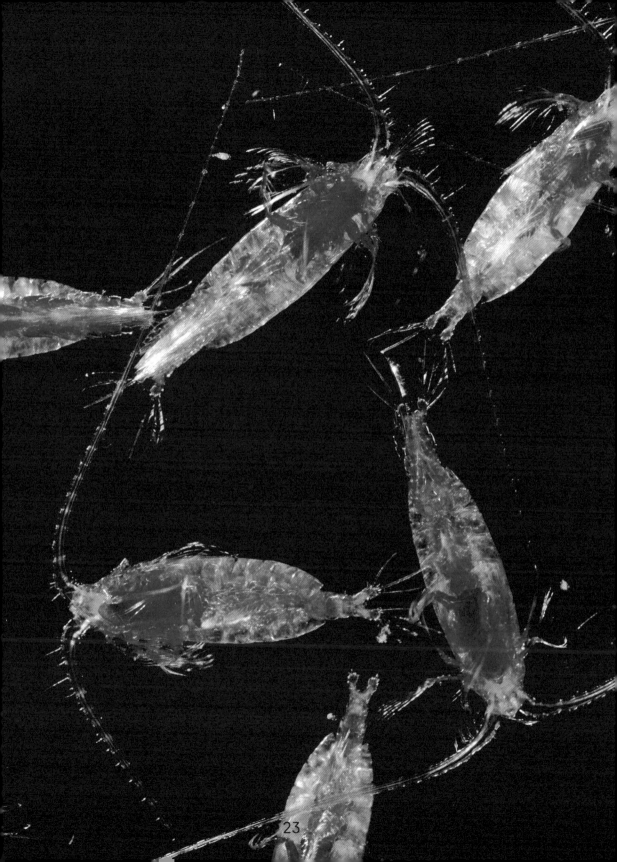

Small Arctic Char

There are different sizes of Arctic char. Small Arctic char are the third link in the Lake Hazen food chain. They live in Lake Hazen all year long. In winter, they live under the ice.

Small Arctic char in Lake Hazen eat copepods.

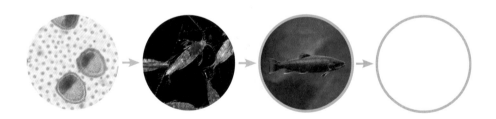

Large Arctic Char

The final link in the Lake Hazen food chain is large Arctic char. Unlike the small Arctic char, large Arctic char need a meal bigger than copepods. Large Arctic char eat smaller Arctic char, even though they are the same species!

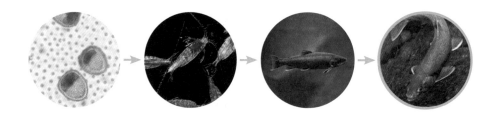

Just like in the Bylot Island food chain, each of the links in the Lake Hazen food chain is connected. If any of the links are taken out, it would affect the other living things in the chain.

For example, if the lake became polluted and algae couldn't grow, then there would be nothing for copepods to eat. Without food, the copepods would disappear. And without copepods to eat, the Arctic char would also disappear.

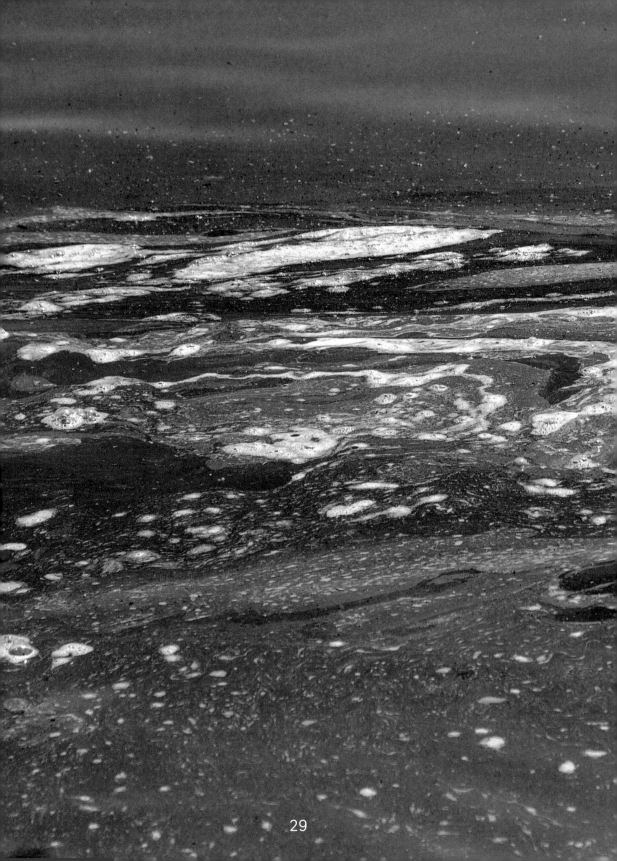

Food chains show how living things depend on each other to survive.

Think about the Bylot Island and Lake Hazen food chains. When we removed one link in the food chain, all the other links were affected. This shows how all living things are connected.

Bylot Island

Lake Hazen

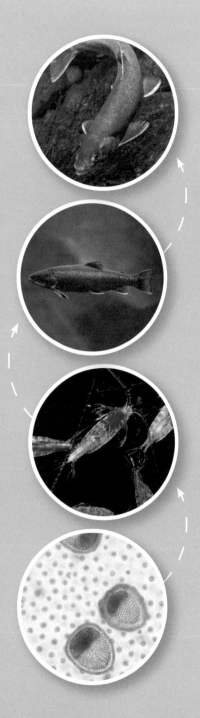